ENGAGEMENT INTERACTION CONVERSION

SOCIAL MEDIA MARKETING
DECODED

HARSHAJYOTI DAS

Dedication

To my readers who have always supported me

About the Author

Harshajyoti Das

Harsh is the CEO and Co-Founder of Munmi IT Solutions LLP.

He is a traveler, a writer, an inbound marketer, an entrepreneur, and a business adviser.

His other books, "How to write content that converts 600% More" and "No SEO Forever" are both bestsellers. He has published over 5 books and is writing his 6th book.

He is also the founder of FireYourMentor.com, a platform for self-published authors.

LET'S CONNECT!

Contact Info:

- **Fan Email:** author@harsh.im

- **Interview/guestposting/Press requests:** press@harsh.im

- **Amazon Author Profile:** http://www.amazon.com/author/harshajyotidas

- **Twitter:** http://twitter.com/jr_sci

- **Facebook:** https://www.facebook.com/harshajyotidas.author

- **LinkedIn:** http://in.linkedin.com/pub/harshajyoti-das/17/28b/52b

- **Google+:** https://plus.google.com/+HarshajyotiDas

Author Website: Harsh.Im

CEO at Munmi IT Solutions LLP:
Munmi.org

Founder of: FireYourMentor.com

Table of Contents

INTRODUCTION

PINTEREST
Advantages of using Pinterest for Business
Actionable Pinterest Tips to Increase Sales and Conversion
A Few Fun Facts about Pinterest
Grow Your Blog Using Pinterest

TWITTER
Twitter For Your Business
Interact Better With Their Audience on Twitter
A Few Twitter Hashtag Tracking and Analytics Tools
Increase Your Blog Retweets On Twitter

GOOGLE+
Essential Tips To Use Google+ Effectively
   Let's Talk About Increasing Google+ Engagement
Google+ Tools to Improve Your Marketing

FACEBOOK
Market Your Brand on Facebook
Some Facebook Predictions for 2014
How Facebook Has Changed The World?
Some Amazing Facebook Advertising Tips

A Note to My Readers

ALSO BY THE AUTHOR

How To Write Content That Converts 600% More

http://amzn.to/1niszm5

ENGAGEMENT INTERACTION CONVERSION

http://amzn.to/1sWn9yB

ZERO ADVERTISING COST BLOG COMMENTING ROCKS

http://amzn.to/1rk4tej

THE ART OF BOOK MARKETING

http://amzn.to/1pcYOU5

BE THE GENIUS YOU WERE BORN TO BE

http://amzn.to/1onMX8C

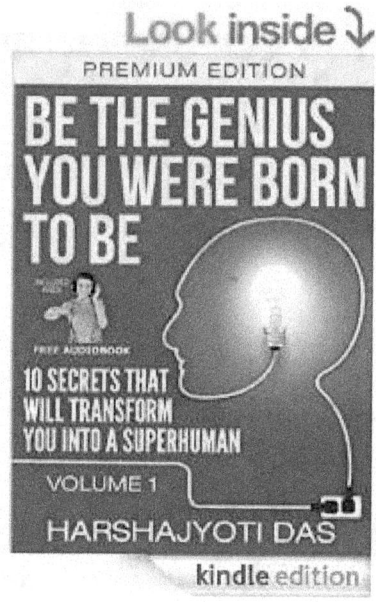

INTRODUCTION

Since you have purchased this book, it proves that you want to earn more traffic from social networks. This is actually the second book of the series "NO SEO FOREVER." You can find the first book here:
http://www.amazon.com/dp/B00LK2SR5M

Google has run multiple algorithmic updates and SEO is nearly dead. We are all looking for alternate traffic sources. What's better than social media traffic? It's free and viral traffic. Social media has totally changed the face of the advertising world in the past few years. Although, since more and more businesses are increasingly using social media to drive traffic to their websites/products, it has become extremely important that we follow the best practices we can put our hands on.

This book is a collection of simple tips and techniques that will help you increase your social media marketing efforts. I have briefly explained each tip so that it's easy for you to remember. Treat this book as a guidebook or a reference book whenever you start a social media campaign. I am sure it will increase the effectiveness of your endeavors by more than 600%.

Some folks might not agree with me when I talk about automating a few steps. We all are different and have different tastes. If you are not a fan of automation like me, please disregard that portion and move on to the next part where I talk about doing it manually.

I recommend some softwares in this book, solely because I have used them and have seen good results in the past.

So who am I?

I am a retired internet marketer with seven years of experience. I started internet marketing when I was a teen. I have helped over 1000 businesses with their online marketing efforts. Now I am a full-time author.

In this book, we will cover the four main social media networks, namely Pinterest, Twitter, Facebook and Google+.

I have read a couple of social media books in the past and they cover very basic information such as "how to open an account", "how to set up a Facebook Campaign" etc. Even after reading 300 pages, they won't come to the point. I won't name these books but after reading them, I felt that I have wasted my time reading pretty basic information that I already know.

The concept behind writing this book is to skip these introductory lessons and directly come to the point. Watch some Youtube tutorials if you want to learn about these basic stuffs. It will save time, money and you will learn sooner.

I value your time and thus I have made this book as concise as possible. I won't talk about how to open a social media account but as to how you can use these four popular social networks to interact, engage and convert better.

Alright, let's get started!

Chapter 1

PINTEREST

Before I go any further, I will show you the power of Pinterest.

Last updated: August 17, 2014

Tracking ID Summary for garccambfat-20

Displaying only the 2 of your 8 tracking IDs that have clicks.

August 16, 2014 to August 17, 2014

Tracking ID	Clicks	Items Ordered	Items Shipped	Shipped Items Revenue	Advertising Fees
penigmabookstore-20	4	0	0	$0.00	$0.00
pinterest0a6d-20	948	0	0	$0.00	$0.00
TOTALS	952	0	0	$0.00	$0.00

The above screenshot shows that Pinterest sent approximately **1000 visitors to** my Amazon affiliate products **within one day**. Now, it's true that Pinterest traffic will not convert as good as paid traffic, but who the hell cares? It's FREE traffic without any work.

Here's another screenshot of a product I am promoting via Pinterest. The conversion is around 1% to 2%, which isn't bad at all.

Traffic Statistics

Visitors	626
Unique Visitors	479
Approved Sales	13
Sales Ratio	2.077%

What if I told you I generated this traffic all on autopilot? I do not spend two to three hours a day on Pinterest, nor do I spend 5 minutes every day. It's all automated. I put aside one to two hours per week to go through my Pinterest account and personalize it a bit. But other than that, it's an automated system that has been constantly driving traffic to me day in and day out.

If you are not a fan of automation, you will have to spend two to three hours every day or hire a VA to do the job.

I use a software called "Pin Blaster, which cost me a one-time fee of $67.00. I have created a video tutorial on how to use the software here: http://fireyourmentor.com/pinblaster-review/

Alternatively, you can use any of the many Pinterest marketing software available in the market.

Pinterest is a social platform where users can collect and put up pictures of all things they love, in one place.

It is used by people all over the world to share photos of things they have made or would like to make. From crafts to DIYs, from recipes to fashion - everything under the sun seems to be available on Pinterest.

Pinterest was founded by Ben Silbermann, Paul Sciarra and Evan Sharp in 2010. After four years, it is now one of the most popular social media sites. Its growth rate has been impressive. It has become the world's fourth largest traffic source and drives more traffic than LinkedIn, Google Plus and even YouTube. Most of Pinterest's users (about 80%) are women.

Also, 30% of the women who use Pinterest are between the ages of 25 and 34 years. The followers you have, the more likes, comments and "pins" you get. Whether you are a new user or an old, use Pinterest to showcase your hobby or as a means to expose your brand.

Use the following 15 tips to increase your Pinterest engagement:

1.   Username and Profile name

The username you choose should describe your profession or interest, as people look for images using specific keywords. People generally do not search for the name of the business or the company unless it is a well-known business. Similarly, your profile name should include the name of the business or the company, along with a user-friendly keyword.

2.   Active Pinterest user

Just having a Pinterest account will not help you. You should be an active user. You should "Like." "re-pin" and "comment" on pins that you like. This is what happens if you are active:

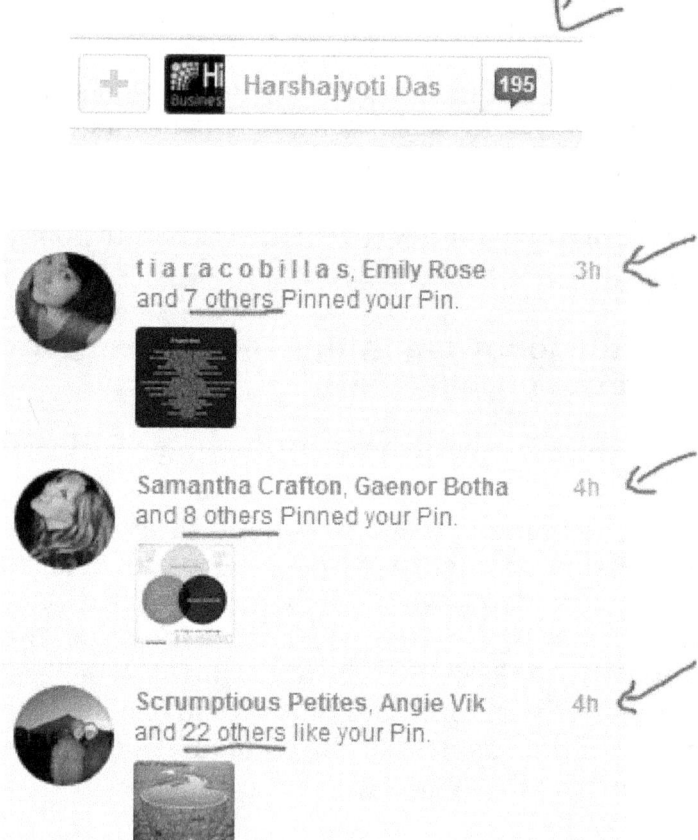

3. Share/Pin images

You can upload images on Pinterest, but it's recommended that you share or re-pin others' images. Find pictures related to your area of interest and pin them to your Pinboard. More than 80% of daily pins are re-pins.

4. Comment on popular "pins:

Commenting on other users' pins will increase your visibility and help you gain more followers. Comment thoughtfully on others' pins.

5. Create group boards

You can invite other people with similar interests to pin on your board and create a Group Board. A group board increases the number of your followers. Your followers, along with the other person's followers, will be able to see your pins. This will thus increase traffic on your board, which in turn will increase the exposure of your board. This will help you to gain further followers.

6. Profile widgets

You can also install a profile widget on your blog or webpage. A profile widget is a collage of 30 of your latest pins. It helps people quickly assess your areas of interest rather than going through all your Pinboards and finding out what your interests are. People with similar interests will then follow you.

7. Customer focused Pinboards

This is for people who use Pinterest to sell their products. You should create Pinboards which focus more on the customers' choices and interests rather than your personal ones. Customers referred by Pinterest are about 10% more likely to buy your products or brands than they are from referrals from any other social networking sites, including Facebook and Twitter. Don't forget to put a price ($xx) on your image if you are selling a product.

8. Add a Pinterest follow button

If you have a website or a blog, you can use the Pinterest follow button to direct traffic to your Pinboard. Place the Pinterest follow button at strategic points all over your website or blog - at the top of the page, on the side and at the bottom where people would normally enter their comments.

9. Ask for opinions

This tip is again for sellers on Pinterest. You can put up images of prototypes of your products and ask your customers to comment on them. With the help of their opinions, your products' quality will improve and you will be able to gain more followers as well.

10. Pin customer's pictures

Ask your customers to send in pictures of them using or wearing your products and brands. This will help you to attract newer and prospective customers.

11. Host contests

Conduct contests on Pinterest and give away freebies to the winners of the contest. This way, you can attract more followers.

12. Promote individual boards

In the midst of all your boards, try to promote individual boards too. This will help to attract people who would be interested in one particular board of products and not the other boards.

13. Follow

This is a cardinal rule for all social networking sites. If you want followers, then you should be ready to follow others. Find and follow others with similar interests as yours.

14. Connect your other social networks

Link multiple social media accounts to your Pinterest account. This way you will be able to tweet about a new "pin" or update your latest Pinterest activity on Facebook and your "followers" and friends will be able to follow you on Pinterest also. More than 2 million Facebook users have connected their Pinterest account to their Facebook timeline.

15. PR Strategy

Some organizations use Pinboards as a public relations strategy. They pin images of various picnics, talent shows, etc. which they have conducted for their employees, in order to increase the publicity of their organization.

These are just a few tried and tested ways in which you can increase the engagement on your Pinterest account. Another way for you to increase your engagement can be to observe when the maximum number of users is active and try to pin your images during those times.

In the end, it is up to each individual to work out different combinations of methods which would help them to increase the traffic on their Pinterest accounts. Pinterest is one of the best ways to increase your digital presence and is one of the most powerful tools in the field of digital marketing.

You just need to work your way around the site, learn its secrets and use it to your maximum benefit.

My personal strategy:

It's nothing out of the ordinary but let me share it with you. I can tell you that it works from from my own personal experiences. I want my readers to use the same strategy and make the best use of it. So, here it is:

1. Find pins in your niche that have received over 50 repins. I do it via the software, Pinblaster but you can do it manually as well. Just search for your keyword on Pinterest or check out popular boards. If you run out of pins, then find pins that have received at least ten repins. Since I can afford to do it in bulk, I keep a lower limit of three repins. Something's better than nothing.

Via the software:

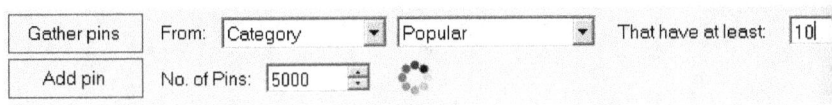

Manually:

1. You need to create separate boards for each niche. For example, I have a couple of different boards for book, SEO, quotes, motivation, etc.
2. While repinning it, you can rename the URL that points from your pin. Whenever somebody clicks on an image, he will be taken to that link. It can include a link to your affiliate page, product page, YouTube video or your sales page.

Via the software:

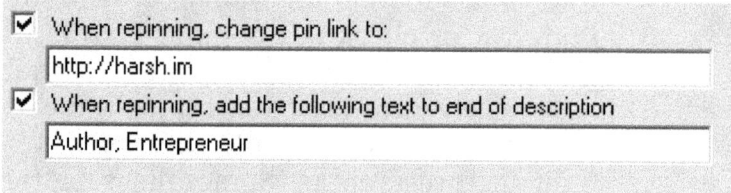

Manually:

On an average, I repin approximately 100 images via the software. I follow the 80/20 rule. Hence, I prefer to repin instead of commenting or liking other pins. You can set aside one day per week to post comments or like other pins. You main focus should be to repin as many pins as possible. Increase the size of your board.

Statistically speaking (from my personal experience), for every 2000 repins, you will receive 100 followers for your board.

In the next chapter, we will talk about how businesses are increasingly using Pinterest to promote themselves.

Chapter 2

Advantages of using Pinterest for Business

Using Pinterest has many advantages in general, and can be of great use to businesses too! You can create pins about your work, your products, etc., and others can repin them to their boards.

Showcases your products through visual data

Pinterest lets you display your product in the form of pictures on your board. You can create a virtual page (Pinboard) just for your products, where you can give post pictures, videos, how-to tips, etc. This attracts the attention of people who search for related content and are directed to or receive the suggestion from your pin board. They can then pin these to their board or like and share them. Your business thus gains brand value and reaches potential clients through sharing.

It is free and promotes your brand on a bigger platform

Pinterest helps you promote your product and your business for free. Plus, it does it through social media, which is the most commonly used platform for interaction. Since pins can be linked to most other social media platforms and shared through them, they reach a vast number of people. It does the job for free, while advertising uses huge amounts of money. Remember one thing; more than half a billion of the advertising industry is moving online. There's a huge advantage to using viral marketing methods instead of paid advertising.

Market research through Pinterest

By tracking the trends on Pinterest, a business can modify its products accordingly. A business can track the changes in user preferences, the changes in the type of pins that are shared, what fashion trends are followed (tracked via the nature of pins related to these topics that are re-pinned). It can then use these ideas to design or modify its own products and services and pins to gain more popularity.

Categories or themed boards

Pinterest allows users to create different categories for different types of content. A brand with different products, for example, can have one board for every product. A business that engages in different fields can have one board for each field. This is a benefit to businesses as they can organize their content and personalize each themed board. It is also a benefit for clients, as they can like the boards they are interested in, instead of the whole business and all of its boards.

Create an exclusive business account

Pinterest has the unique option of creating business accounts, and even personal accounts can be converted into business accounts.

Pinterest is therefore one of the best social media platforms for businesses due to its business-specific features. Your visual content also adds credibility and brand value. It easily connects with other sites and is perfect for sharing information on a large scale.

A lot of businesses are already harnessing the power of Pinterest. If you own a business, it's high time you look into finding some time to add a Pinterest marketing strategy to your agenda.

In the next chapter, I will offer some quick and essential tips, mainly for small business owners, to increase conversion and sales. Even if you are an individual, you will find them useful.

Chapter 3

Actionable Pinterest Tips to Increase Sales and Conversion

Shopper's inspirations thrive on the pins. With Pinterest being a visually-oriented social network, users are likely to make comparatively better purchases. You can grab some of these creative marketing techniques to market your products better! Let's dive into the ocean of Pinterest marketing and swim around with the techniques for a while.

Visual Aesthetics:

By Visual aesthetics I mean kick-ass photography and tricks. You see, Pinterest is visual social media; you should be confident in how you handle presenting your products. That sure plays a vital role. Let me give you some pointers here.

Background: Plain white and light gray works just great, as it will highlight your products better. I would say "keep it simple."

Lighting: Avoid extreme lighting. Pale lighting and medium lighting can get you more repins, visitors and conversions!

Editing:

Texture: Play it smooth. Smooth is in! Bland and smooth textures will make your product stand out.

Colors: Mix colors. Make sure your image has multiple dominant colors. These colors should blend with the background. This can get you more repins.

Now you will have your own eye-catching image of your products. Make sure you read through a few blogs and tutorials before you get started on these tips.

Giveaways:

Can you tell me one person who doesn't like giveaways? I absolutely love them. Make sure you produce a giveaway page and link it right to your Pinterest. People adore giveaways. It may only be a small kit of supplies or a tutorial, but they will surely pin your page and you will get more repins, especially if you have a pin-it button on your page. Duh!

Graze through:

Look out for actions like "sign up" and "join our list" to see what other businesses are doing. Once you sign up, I am pretty sure you will be able to come up with a lot more ideas from their work. It is always best to take a peek into others' works.

Let's talk Infographics:

Let me tell you this; no one likes reading stats, so to make it interesting, put it up as an image with little illustrations. In other words, make an infographic explanation. Infographics are very popular on Pinterest. Be sure that your stunning infographics talk about a particular problem and how your product will sort out that problem. Make sure that the infographics are visually appealing. Also, another thing about stats; if you have a great stat, it will surely encourage people to buy your product.

Life is more than products:

Of course! It's more than just products, isn't it? Make sure you give small tips and tidbits that can be linked to your pins directly. These small tips make a huge difference on Pinterest. If the tip is something that's catchy, it will spread around like wild fire. Thank me later!

Reach out:

Make sure you stay in touch with your fans and also touch your fans. By touch your fans, I mean ask them for a picture of your product being used, and pin it on your business page. This can fetch a few more friends of your fans. For example, if you are marketing clothes, make sure you get a great picture of them wearing it.

Video phase on!

Okay! You will have to give the customers a video treat. This gets viral quite easily. Bring people to life and explain how amazingly your product solves their problem. Remember, a people's attention span is very short. See that your video is quick and grabs their attention. Also, you can share your video tutorials.

Discounts, festive sales and gifts:

Offer discounts with an appealing product photo. Now, people will not only see your products, but also your discounts. Make sure you offer them during festive peaks, for instance about ten days before Christmas. Distribute gifts during the festive season and make sure that you mention free gifts along with your product images. This will potentially generate more sales, since people are naturally attracted to discounts and freebies.

Portfolio Board:

Please have an interesting portfolio board of your products. See to it that you edit your "Source URL" for your pins and link them to your landing page.

Hits on Testimonials:

Turn your customer testimonials into fancy quoted images, and then pin them to your testimonial boards. Link the testimonials to your particular product or service. You should also post quick video testimonials on your testimonial boards.

Run Contests:

Create exciting contests. Make poster images and pin them. Make sure you offer exciting gifts with the contests. Share the contests with your regular customers and fans. This will also make an impact.

The bottom-line is that Pinterest is a visually-oriented social media channel. To reach an audience, it is all about posting visually appealing entries. Therefore, take your time and create some awesome visuals that will string the shoppers in.

Get to work and create those amazing visuals. Good luck!

Chapter 4

A Few Fun Facts about Pinterest

I have to agree, most of the clients who come to me for social media consulting are mostly on Twitter and Facebook. When I mention Pinterest to them, they are like, *"Is it worth my time to create a marketing strategy for Pinterest? Facebook is already working for me."* I need to reassure them that although Pinterest is the youngest of all social media, it has grown exponentially in the past few years. It's a honey pot for traffic for your business, if you take it seriously.

The world is buzzing about Pinterest. Trust me, a few of these awesome facts will make you sign up for Pinterest. For those already on Pinterest, this will be a mind-boggling surprise. This visual discovery tool has about 70 million users and this count keeps climbing. I strongly believe Pinterest is going to last way longer, since users seem to just love it. Better late than never; these are the few things about Pinterest you should know.

Pinterest drives queen-sized referential traffic:

Pinterest became the second largest traffic source in the world as of June 2014, and this means Pinterest is directly trailing Facebook. Pinterest sends more referral traffic than Twitter, Google+, Reddit, Stumbleupon, YouTube, Linkedin, and Tumblr combined!

Leading sources of worldwide social media referral traffic in June 2014, by share of visits

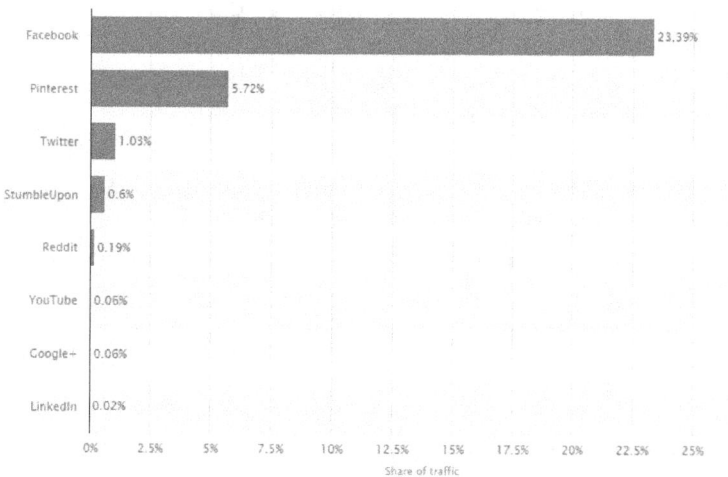

Source:
http://www.statista.com/statistics/235575/leading-internet-referral-traffic-sources/

Heads up to popularity:
Pinterest is the fastest growing independent site in the history. (source:

http://techcrunch.com/2012/02/07/pinterest-monthly-uniques/)

The site falls in the category of the fifth most popular social networks in the world. Pinterest currently gets about 41 million unique visitors every month. Don't be surprised!

Number of unique U.S. visitors to Pinterest.com from January 2011 to July 2014 (in millions)

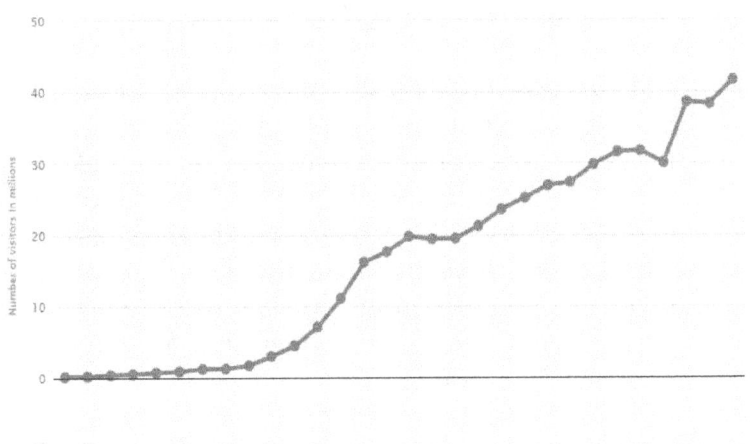

Source:
http://www.statista.com/statistics/277694/number-of-unique-us-visitors-to-pinterestcom/

iPad users and their love for Pinterest:
Pinterest is highly popular among iPad users. Facebook may be dominating the iPhone users,

but 50% of iPad users are being dominated by Pinterest.

Time and addiction is directly proportional:
Pinterest drives the user to browse the site for about one hour per month (on average), which is much longer than compared to Facebook. The average browsing time for Facebook is about 12 minutes. Pinterest is highly viral; more so than any other social network. It is approximately three times more effective than Twitter.

Is Pinterest a chick thing?
Statistical data tells us more than half of Pinterest users are women. So it is a chick thing right? Well, maybe not. That is an old story. Pinterest is widely used by both sexes, but women just love it. Pinterest was developed by three male co-founders; it was intended to help with stamp and shoe collections. So guys, it is not merely a chick thing.

Unlike post updates, pins never die:
The life expectancy of the pin tends to last longer than a status update on Facebook or a tweet. An average tweet lasts for few minutes before it gets rushed out by a bunch of other tweets. Similarly, on Facebook a status update lasts for a few hours before it vanishes. But Pinterest pins are like a never-ending story. Once users begin searching for pins, they uncover and resurrect more pins, including the older pins.

I opened www.ViralDojo.com as a test to check the power of Pinterest. The prime sources of traffic are Google and Pinterest. No manual job was involved. It was 100% on auto pilot (from posting articles to re-pinning).

Here's how the test went:

Started Viraldojo.com : May 17, 2014
Stopped Working on Viral Dojo: July 26, 2014
Traffic as of September 2014: 21,507 unique visitors (13k from Google and 3.3k from Pinterest).

Even now, the site gets approx 20-30 visitors from Pinterest, even though we stopped pinning back in July.

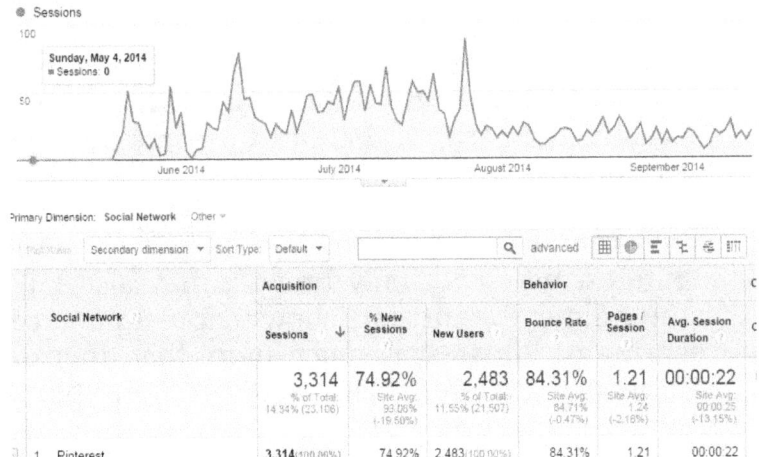

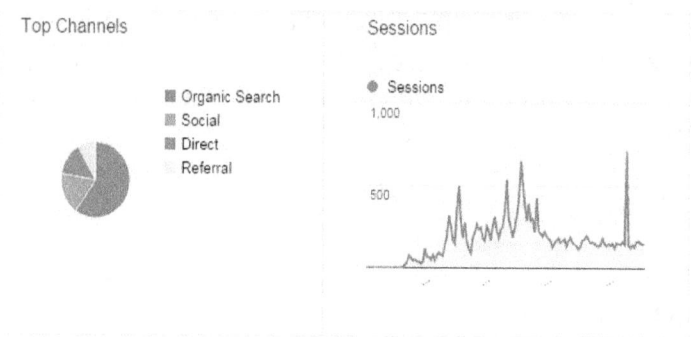

As you can see, I am still getting traffic for the work done around two months back. Name one social media network that has the same lifetime as Pinterest.

Buying and Pinterest:
Pinterest users not only browse, they also buy stuff online. Recent stats show that e-commerce sharing of Pinterest is much more than that of Facebook. Pinterest user spends more bling online.

Site categories with the highest concentration of Pinterest visitors in 2nd quarter 2012

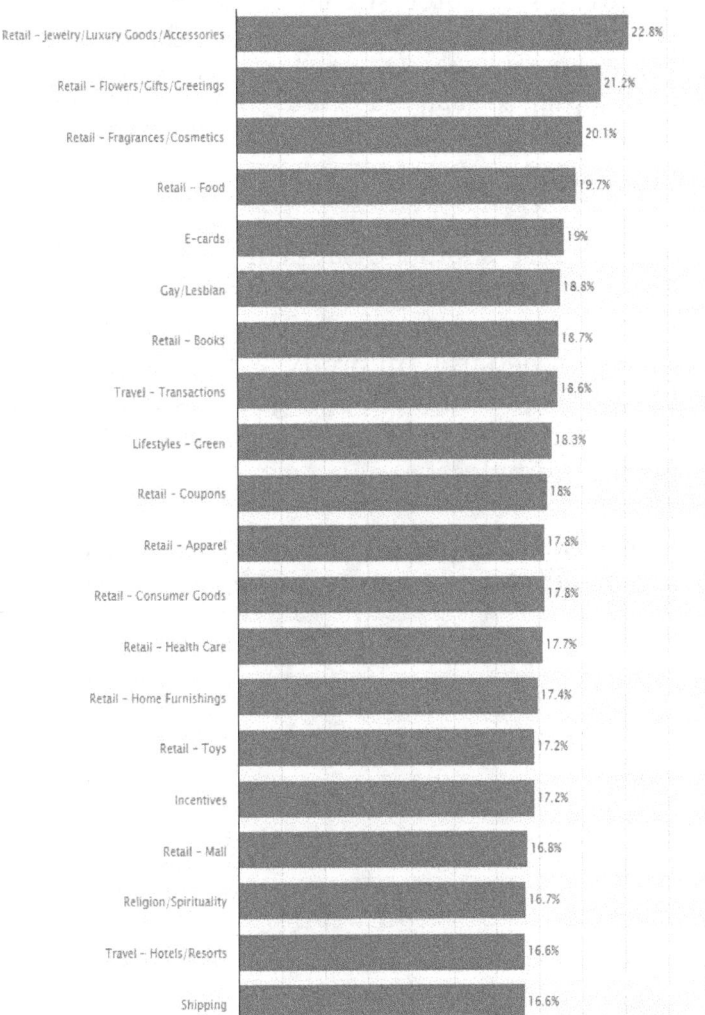

Pinterest and fundraising:

Pinterest has raised about $338 million in fundraising. Pinterest raised the funds globally, which includes France, England and Italy. Pinterest has also shown interest in connecting with Japan as well.

So, there you go . . .

If Pinterest should disappear one day, I don't know if I would be able to survive in my pre-Pinterest, un-crafty life with no desserts. Been there, pinned it. I am pretty sure it would be real hard. Now, I suggest you get to work on your Pinspiration with some help from Pinterest. Start pinning!

In the next chapter, we will learn how a blogger can use Pinterest to grow his blog.

Chapter 5

Grow Your Blog Using Pinterest

If you have had an idea, any idea, or even a thought that took total possession of your mind, and all you wanted was to reach out, spill it, get it heard, then you must have already opted for the virtual world. And if you haven't already, well don't waste your time reading this any further. Let's just say you are way behind, for lack of better words.

For those of you who are already a part of the blogosphere, and started blogging for whatever reason, be it personal or professional, chances are that you don't have more than say 1000 visitors per month and have already toned down your original intentions. And why wouldn't you? You are competing with millions.

Don't fool yourself into believing that you will get started with it right away. You must start with the simple step of writing content, then add some more content, and if you have noticed no hike in traffic, maybe you have written more articles. If you have done so and haven't received the desired results, then let us be clear. The fact that you are jotting some more content won't do you much good. What will help you is making use of the content you already have, that is, to make sure your present content is being noticed. How? This is where Pinterest comes to your rescue.

Pinterest allows you to save, upload and manage photos, called pins. Users can browse through the pins of others and pin them up or add their own pins to their own Pinboard. To be more accurate, chances are that your viewers will double if you use Pinterest.

Here's a general idea:

You or your readers pin 1000 images from your website every month, and then 10%, or 100 pins, are repinned by somebody else. Approximately 50% of these pins will receive more than 5 repins. This equals to 100/2 x 5 = 250 repins. Again, 50% of those repins are again repinned by even more people. This equals to 250/2 x 5 = 625 repins. The reach continues and your pins will be visible to more and more people every day.

And where will each repin link to? YOUR WEBSITE!

Remember the three P's (Pin, Post, Pic)

Pin the posts on your blog with pics. Take an example and ask yourself this - would you prefer reading a verbose description of a blog promoting a certain apparel brand or would you prefer read it with a glimpse of some of their collection? The latter is preferable, no doubt, so you better provide the viewers with not just content to read, but content they can also look at.

Making pics accessible and handy

Who likes complexities? No one. Make it clear and easy for visitors to make their way to your Pinboard. Drop a link of that pic in your blog. Add a "pin it" button on every photo on your blog so that people can pin and re-pin your photos. After all, pinning and repinning is what it's all about. Do you see a cycle here?

For Wordpress, you can use a plug-in called "Image Sharer" by Sumome.com, which can place a social sharing button on every image on your website. It will stay invisible until someone hovers their mouse over the image. You can try this out on my site, http://fireyourmentor.com/, to see how it works.

It is worth pinning pics, and doing so chronically

No one has enough time to spare on just any other photo. Give them a reason to rest their eyes on your pic and pin it on their own board. Make it worth pinning and re-pinning. How? Well, be specific. For example, if you blog about fine dinnerware, then direct the users to a pic focusing on the brand of the dinnerware and its design, not on the food in it. Also, it's better to provide a pic chronically for each step. For example, posting a pic after every step of a recipe is a good idea.

Well framed board name and description

Users pin their photos on Pinboards with a name and description. Suppose you were able to draw the attention of a viewer on your photo. Then what? If you aroused some curiosity in this view, he or she would continue reading the description. Write it in such a way that the reader doesn't regret waiting by your pic just to end up reading something not interesting. Users may also view the original source of the pic.

Biased to certain pics? Pin on multiple boards.

There is a chance that you want certain photo to get noticed, but the board you have categorized it in may not have a lot of followers or visibility. A little bit of cheating here won't harm anybody. You can simply pin this particular pic on more than just one board, even when it doesn't strictly comes under that category.

Return the favor!
Don't you appreciate it when someone reciprocates for you, for instance they give you a candy in return for a candy? Certainly you do. So, if you have some consistent people following up and pinning your photos, be generous enough to spend some time viewing their pins and pinning those that are worthy to be on your board. Remember, the *rule of reciprocation* goes a long way.

Keep track of your popular pics, and bad ones too!
Stay informed about photos that earned you great exposure and try coming up with something similar every now and then.

Go to http://pinterest.com/source/YOURBLOGURLHERE.com and find out what people are pinning from your blog. Keep track of your "not so popular" images as well. Be smart, and get rid of them if needed.

Business blogs? Host a contest!
Statistics reveal that Pinterest helped business blogs increase their traffic to soaring levels. What they did was organize a contest. In such contests you can ask visitors to pin content from your blog to their Pinboards or pin something that leads them back to your blog. Then, choose the person whose pinning activities gave your blog the maximum exposure as the winner. Everybody loves contests!

Pinterest via Facebook and Twitter apps. Do it all!
If you are leaving no stone unturned to grow your blog with Pinterest, you need to make sure people can access your Pinboards in all possible ways. Squeeze in your Pinterest links on every social networking site you are on. Add it to your Facebook timeline and on Twitter. What else? Get the Pinterest cell phone app. Stay updated.

Pin what you like. Let them know you
If you are blogging for interacting and not business purposes, you must have pinned what you like, your interests. But if latter is the case, you still should not be strictly confined to business-related pins. Open up. Let them know a

little bit. It doesn't have to be too much, but people always like to know the person behind the desk.

Here's one more trick I use with my Wordpress blogs.

I use a plug-in called "Wordpress Pinterest Automatic."

You will find it here: http://deandev.com/wppinterest/ .

This plug-in will automatically pin all your images from your blog to Pinterest. I am a big fan of automation, but if you prefer to do it manually, go ahead. As it is, it won't take much of your time.

Follow these simple steps and don't forget to be patient. Pinterest is huge. It takes time and effort to build anything. Now, this is a universal truth, isn't it?

Chapter 6

TWITTER

Twitter is a social networking and microblogging website used by millions of people worldwide.

It was created and launched in 2006 by Jack Dorsey, Biz Stone, Noah Glass and Evan Williams. Twitter enables its users to posture "Tweets" consisting of only 140 characters. I'm sure you are already aware of it, but I am still mentioning it because some of my readers are 60-year-olds who are unfamiliar with any social networking sites.

Like any other social networking site, Twitter allows its users to "follow" other users and also to be "followed." A user's popularity is determined by the number of "followers" a person has.

Here are 15 tricks for you to gain more "followers" and increase your engagement on Twitter.

1. Complete your Bio. It is important for you to fill in your public details so that it becomes easier for other users to look for you and find you. It is easier to look up a user when most of her or his details are posted, as it makes matching the search criteria much faster.

2. Remain active
No one will want to follow you if your Twitter remains inactive for a long time, unless you are a world famous celebrity. Send out at least two to three tweets every day, but be sure that your tweets are meaningful. In this case, quality matters more than quantity. I would recommend a couple of tweets every hour. Automate a few tweets if you have to. I will talk about automation late in this chapter.

3. "Follow" other users
Now, here's the most important trick for you to take away from this chapter on Twitter. *The*

more you follow others, the more others will follow you. It's how it works with Twitter.

If you would like your Twitter to be followed, you need to "follow" others too. Begin by "following" famous influencers in your niche. You can also follow people who follow one of your influencers. This way, they will start following you as well. After that, start following people who share the same interests as you do. When you start "following" them, your username pops up when other users "follow" the same person. In other words, Twitter will recommend that they follow you since you share the same interests or you follow the same people. Thus, people with similar interests will start "following"
you.

How much is too much?

Well, I would recommend you to follow at least 100-200 people per day.

<u>Let's do the math:</u>

By the end of 30 days, you would have followed 3000-6000 people, and by the end of a year, you would have followed 40,000-80,000 people. Even if only 50% of them begin to follow you, you will have 20,000-40,000 followers by the end of the year. To be honest, it's always more than 50%. For some of my clients, I have seen almost 60% to 70% begin to follow them back.

Persistence and consistency is the key!

Don't overdo it. Twitter has started banning tons of fake accounts.

4. Share links
It is important that you publicize your interests to attract other like-minded users. Share links of various informative and interesting articles. If you like animals and you are against animal cruelty, share articles or videos which will make your stand on that particular cause clearer and stronger.

Your primary focus should be on becoming an authority in your niche.

5. Put up images
A picture is worth a thousand words. Visual content attracts more attention than just words. Upload various interesting and visually-appealing images to engage the minds of your "followers." Studies have shown that images engage the attention of four to five times more people than just simple text.

6. Interact with your "followers"
It is not just enough to have numerous "followers." You need to interact with them too.

Say "Hello" to a new follower. Thank "followers" who have retweeted your tweets and links. Reply to people who have responded to your tweets. Your interaction with your "followers" shows that you are an approachable person and people would obviously like to "follow" a helpful and friendly person rather than an unfriendly and grumpy person.

You do not need to do it daily. Set aside one day a week (say Sunday) to check out https://twitter.com/i/notifications)

7. Schedule your tweets

You might have followers from all over the world, but it is physically impossible for you to keep tweeting whenever they are active. You can make use of apps like Tweetadder, Buffer, Tweetdeck, Twuffer, Later Bro, Twaitter, FutureTweets, etc. to keep your followers engaged even when it is the middle of the night for you. These apps help you to schedule your tweets for different times of the day. You can schedule your tweet for time when you may be busy in a meeting or when you are taking care of some other important task. Personally, I use Tweetadder as my Twitter Marketing Software. I have created a tutorial on how to use TweetAdder here: http://fireyourmentor.com/twitter-guide

8. Retweet

If you want people to retweet your tweets, you should start retweeting too. Add some value to your retweet to make it stick out in the crowd. Adding a short comment like "Must read!" or "Please Rewteet" or "Comment Below" will make your retweet stand out among all the others. Do not hesitate to ask your "followers" for retweets. Be upfront.

9. Use short and crisp tweets
The shorter the tweet, the better it is. Though Twitter allows a maximum of 140 characters in each of its tweets, it is better to use less. Research has shown that tweets with 70 to 120 characters are retweeted the most.

10. Use Hashtags
Hashtags (#) are one of the most important features of Twitter. A hashtag brings all the similar tweets together. Hashtags can be used for special words or small catch phrases. Too many hashtags in a single tweet will harm your tweet rather than make it popular. Do not use more than two hashtags per tweet. People can search inside Twitter for a particular trend. If you use #hashtag, you are increasing your chance to get discovered.

11. Link your other social network profiles
Almost all of us have accounts on multiple social networks. Link all of your profiles to your

Twitter account so that your Facebook friends or your Google+ circles can start following you on Twitter as well.

12. Start a conversation
Start conversations with people who you think might have similar interests as you do. Ask questions which can be answered with a "Yes" or a "No" or in one word. Answer other peoples questions. This is a good way to start a conversation in Twitter which can help you find other people with common interests.

People love to answer when you ask for their opinion on a topic. At the same time, they hate it when you are asking them uncomfortable questions like, "how much do you earn?" You need to know the difference between what to ask and what not to ask.

<u>Let me give you a few examples:</u>

Good questions:
1. What do you think about XYZ (topic) that was on the news recently?
2. I read your article on XYZ. How do you think "your profession" can use it?
3. Where do you see the future of XYZ (any profession, industry)?

Bad questions:

1. *Irrelevant questions:* How much do you earn? How big is your email list?
2. *Personal questions:* Are you married? Are you happy? Do you love your children?
3. *Asking them to share their secrets:* How are you getting clients? What's your marketing strategy?

You also need to note that when an influencer tweets you using @yourusername, it will increase your Klout score.

13. Look out for trending topics
Keep your eyes open to check out what topics are trending at the time you tweet. Not only will your tweets be on the top, it will also make you seem more knowledgeable and involved in your own tweets.

14. Be yourself
Always be yourself. Do not try to pretend you are someone you are not, especially in a virtual platform. You will engage more people's attention if you tweet something funny which has happened to you or someone around you. Most people can find out if you make things up. No one likes fake people, not even in the virtual world.

15. Use quotes

Well, if you really have nothing to tweet, but have an urge to tweet, use famous quotes. I post motivational and business quotes a couple of times throughout the day. They get a lot of retweets. Don't use long and complicated ones.

I hope these secrets help you to unveil the mystery of Twitter and engage more followers. But be warned, it will take time for you to increase your Twitter engagement.

Like the old adage says, "Slow and steady wins the race." You need to steadily build up your Twitter base. Perseverance is the key to finding success there.

How many Twitter Followers do you have? What do you mainly do to earn more followers? I want to hear from my readers. Email me, let's connect!

Chapter 7

Twitter for Your Business

In the era of social networking, sites such as Facebook, Twitter, etc., have been instrumental in boosting businesses. These social networking sites have proven to be one of the best platforms to push businesses forward, as a large number of users compare and negotiate products online. It's also due to the fact that these sites offer an interactive platform where the customers can directly interact with the seller.

Twitter can be used creatively in several ways to promote business. Let's have a look at five ways in which "Twitter chats" can help your business grow.

Attract people by making your profile attractive

The primary strategy to improve your business is creating a profile which will attract the customers. Post attractive pictures, videos and advertisements promoting your business. Make it more interesting by engaging the customers in questionnaire sessions and by conducting polls. James Altucher @jaltucher, a millionaire author, conducts weekly Q & A's every Thursday, in order to interact with his audience. Come up with something like him and it will increase your Twitter engagement.

Initially, offering discounts and freebies can improve your visibility and give you an edge over your competitors. You can also host giveaways on your social media accounts.

Analyze the expectations of the potential buyers

Create an environment where your customers know that you are open to suggestions. Receive feedback and complaints from customers and be prompt in taking the steps necessary to satisfy your customers. Closely monitor the strategies used by your competitors in order to attract the crowd and follow up as quickly as possible so you can take the lead. Have one-on-one personal interaction with customers and maintain a good rapport with them.

Ron Mais @goodcoin316 · Sep 12
@jr_sci Hi Pal! I just got your book No SEO Forever. Can't wait to drive traffic to my site using your info.

FAVORITES
2

9:20 AM - 12 Sep 2014 · Details

Collapse ← Reply ↨ Retweet ★ Favorited ••• More

Reply to @goodcoin316

 Harshajyoti Das @jr_sci · 23h
@goodcoin316 Hey Ron, it's so great to hear from you. Will be mailing you another book on #Socialmedia very soon. Hope you are on my list.
Expand

Identify the right crowd

Identify the people who are keenly interested in your products, whose suggestions will be valuable. Have constant interaction with them to get more ideas. Follow their posts, and re-tweet their posts if they are relevant to your line of business. Create a group of people around you with the same interests to be updated about the latest trends, expectations and ideas for improvement.

Utilize Twitter Ad products

Twitter's Promoted Accounts feature lets you be around the right people who can influence your business. It aims at increasing the number of followers. The users can be targeted by keywords on your timeline - interests, geography, gender, etc. This feature allows you to track your results in real-time. Similarly, the "promoted tweets" feature makes your tweets appear on the timeline of potential followers by analyzing their interests, geography, location, etc. Twitter analytics offers dashboards on your timeline to help you analyze which tweet is attractive to the consumers by tracking down the number of mentions, follows, etc. Moreover, the followers dashboard gives you the opportunity to analyze the location and interests of your audience.

Third party applications

Though twitter offers ad products to analyze your results, things might become a little too hectic when multiple business accounts are involved. Analyzing each dashboard and following up would be impossible. To resolve this issue, third-party applications, which combine all the statistics on one dashboard, are available.

You can check out these Twitter analytical websites:

1. http://www.tweetstats.com
2. http://twittercounter.com/
3. http://www.socialbakers.com/twitter/
4. http://www.twitonomy.com/
5. http://followerwonk.com

These versatile features offered by Twitter have allowed it to play a vital role in marketing and businesses. It has paved the way for the customers to interact and express what they want and how they want it. Twitter has proven to be a very useful platform for businesses to find their potential buyers with fewer hassles, within a shorter span of time. How much of its potential are you using in your business?

Chapter 8

Interact Better With Their Audience on Twitter

Social media is an under-valued entity. While it's most common use is to communicate, its ability to reach a large amount of people is often not given much credit, nor is it put to effective use. This is rather advantageous for small businesses, as they can use this forum to increase their audience, and also make their mark faster and better than their competitors.

Use Hooks

The best way to attract more clients through Twitter is by effectively grabbing their attention. Fun facts, short quizzes, prizes etc. can help do just that. While just tweeting facts about your company might get you little attention, facts from all over the world which are still relevant to your business can do the job right.

Short quizzes can also help you gain personal communication, as the clients will reply to your tweets by giving the answers. For example, a small chocolate business can ask the question, "What is the most important ingredient in chocolate?" and the clients/potential customers will reply with answers. You can offer gift coupons as a prize for the best reply. This will attract even customers to interact with you on Twitter.

Be visual

Share pictures, videos, doodles, cartoons, vines etc. for an easy-on-the-eye approach. Pictures often speak better than words. Videos make the information more comprehensive and reduce the client's effort.

These pictures or videos don't necessarily have to be related to the business. These can even be popular videos or pictures of interest to the community of followers. If a particular pin on Pinterest gets a lot of repins, you can use it on Twitter to engage your Twitter followers. Find what's working and then use it across all channels.

It is important to keep the target audience, which are the followers, in mind and share content that they would be interested in. For example, a start-up garment company can share pictures of their designs, but also pictures of celebrities wearing crazy attire, in order to increase the possibility of being re-tweeted or shared.

Personal Interaction

Nothing attracts customers more than a sense of personal attachment. Re-tweet your followers' tweets, share your thoughts about their tweets with them, and help them find things if they need it. Use their personal Twitter handles and credit them for their activity related to your tweets. Keep the tone conversational and fun. Be their friend. Also use the Twitter handles of your co-workers to ensure their satisfaction. They will feel acknowledged, as will your customers and they will re-tweet you and invite their friends to follow you.

Dell did something similar with me a couple of weeks back. Here's a screenshot.

Harshajyoti Das @jr_sci · Aug 31
A man should never neglect his family for business. - Walt Disney

Dell India @Dell_IN · Sep 1
@jr_sci True that! Here's another one for you! #ConnectedDellSe
pic.twitter.com/UyavCExhYp

Promotions

You can also use Twitter to promote your products. Just Tweet information and back that information with relevant pictures of products (see the screenshot above).

You can use phrases like "guess the name of our new product for skincare" alongside a picture of the product. This again involves personal interaction with the customers. You can even launch new products on this platform. Questions like "Would you like to try it? Reply below" can be used to get an idea of how the public will receive the product.

You can also give offers and discounts and ask people to "like to receive this offer," or tell them to re-tweet the post a certain number of times in order to get a discount. This will further promote the product. They can also be asked to vote for their favorite product, so that the owners know how their products are being received.

Feedback

Once the initial contact with the customers has been established, you can ask them for their direct feedback. Sometimes customers might use your Twitter handle to share experiences - for example - "Checking out the products at @storename." You can then tweet using their handle and ask them if they liked anything. A customer's opinion is of utmost importance.

Questions like "Which new product would you like to see?" or "share your own ideas" or "Did you like our new range of summer products?" can also help gain reviews. Don't just listen, respond to this feedback and assure them that their queries will be answered, complaints will be heard and expectations will be met. Remember to keep a healthy and positive tone.

Be regular and up-to-date

It is of supreme importance to keep up with the latest trends and post content that is relevant to your users. Post about latest issues/news, voice your concern about current topics and show them that you care. It's not all about your business' interests, but also about how well you can engage with your customers' interests.

Keep posting regularly and be active on Twitter. Also, provide important information about your business, like new showrooms, change of locations, new website etc.

When all of these points are kept in mind, social media can become more than a means of entertainment. One thing that start-ups and small businesses often lack is money and they are in constant need of an effective means of promotion. With money an issue and advertisements not being in the budget, social interactions with clients can help a great deal.

Twitter is inexpensive, efficient and a great way to attract more and more customers.

Hashtag has become pretty popular with Twitter. In our next chapter we will talk about a few Hashtag tracking tools that you can use for your business.

Chapter 9

A Few Twitter Hashtag Tracking and Analytics Tools

Hashtag is an efficient element to drive web traffic on Twitter. They ensure that tweets reach a targeted and large audience, so it is important to decide how you use hashtags in your tweets for maximum exposure. What you will need to do is analyze the hashtags you use and use them in your favor. Browse through these six awesome Twitter hashtag and analytics tools to get an idea of how to go about it.

1. **Advanced Twitter Search (https://twitter.com/search-advanced)**
This is a built-in tool in Twitter that helps collect various information based on searches related to hashtags, specific words/phrases, names, tweeple, etc. It provides a comprehensive overview of whatever you are looking for. This simple and free tool is not used by many social media managers, but it provides detail-oriented results. Give it a try.

2. **Hashtagify (http://hashtagify.me/)**
This simple yet effective tool is a craze when tracking hashtags. It provides you with tweets that contain particular hashtags, and also recommends a list of similar hashtags that one can search for. It is the best tool for a beginner in hashtag tracking. It also shows who the top influencers are for a particular hashtag.

3. **Talkwalker (http://www.talkwalker.com/)**
One of my buddies works as a marketing manager in a huge corporation and was recently struggling to find a way to promote their varied products via hashtags on Twitter. He wanted to know exactly the kind of audience he was going to target and also his competitors' reach. Talkwalker came to his rescue. It analyzes content on different social media platforms and blogs beyond the usual tweets, retweets, popularity and influencers. It gives useful insight on the followers of the hashtags based on gender, geographical location and overall sentiment (positive or negative). The results are displayed in easy-to-read charts or the sheets can be imported into MS Excel, PowerPoint or Word.

4. **Tagboard (https://tagboard.com/)**
Tagboard is a tool that is useful in case you are looking for data and analytics of hashtags across

social media platforms above and beyond Twitter. The hashtag you are looking for is searched and analyzed on the various platforms (Twitter, Facebook, Google+, Instagram, App.net, etc.) where it is used. The interface is quite attractive and user-friendly. You can choose just one or any combination of social platforms to track your particular hashtag, so you know where to go in case you have a cross-platform event or a campaign to organize.

5. Hash Tracking (https://www.hashtracking.com/)
One of my previous colleagues, Lynda, was trying to launch a startup. Being new in the market, she had to run a plethora of online media campaigns in the initial days. For the purpose of finding out whether she was actually generating anything from those campaigns and how she should modify them, she used "Hash Tracking." It is a convenient hashtag tracking tool that allows you to not only analyze hashtags based on their users, shared links, conversations, retweets and trending period, but also monitor events and campaigns related to them in real- time.

6. Twubs (http://twubs.com/)
Twubs is a great hashtag tool that gives you the usual tweets, retweets, influencers and trend time of a hashtag. However, what makes it stand out is its range of other features. It provides a

directory of all hashtags used in Twitter. It also acts as a hashtag registry. You can register your hashtag and it will have a specific landing page with all its trend details. What's more, you can even host chat sessions with users following your hashtag and actually connect with them.

Whether you are a high school student, a businessman, a homemaker or a celebrity, you can use one (or more) of these awesome tools to suit your needs and purpose. Never again will you hesitate while using your hashtags, as these tools will help you decide exactly how, when and where to use them.

Happy hashtagging!

Chapter 10

Increase Your Blog Retweets On Twitter

Blogs today are an important and indispensable part of the web. Almost all major businesses have a blog to stay connected with their audience. They are messengers of information, but need to be promoted well in order to achieve their market goals. A big share of their promotions on Twitter can be credited to retweeting of tweets and posts by other users. So, here are some tips and related tools that will help you get your blog posts retweeted to reach a wider audience.

Continue trending with Social Oomph (https://www.socialoomph.com/):

Social Oomph is a tool where one can write and store a pool of tweets. One simply has to update the pool with new content from one's blog regularly. This tool will then continue to tweet and circulate the stored tweets at regular time intervals. You can also choose to make your tweets appear sequentially or randomly. This will allow your blog to keep trending and the content won't be repetitive at the same time.

Time the tweets with Buffer (https://bufferapp.com/):

The Twitter button on your blog page will instantly send out a tweet from a user's account. A better way to increase web traffic is by scheduling the shares you receive from users. Buffer is a tool that can help you do just that. It can help you schedule how your tweets will be spaced throughout the day and/or week. You can also let Buffer time the tweets on its own based on your best exposure time.

Make it easy with ClickToTweet/Easy Tweet Embed/Hrefshare:

https://clicktotweet.com/
https://wordpress.org/plugins/easy-tweet-embed/
http://hrefshare.com/

One of my Facebook buddies, Jose, says that he would never go through the hassle of copying content from a post in order to tweet, even if he finds it interesting. Such is the belief of most people, and we really can't really blame them. A quick fix to this is using tools such as ClickToTweet or Easy Tweet Embed. What ClickToTweet does is that it gives buttons to users to share excerpts that you choose from the post. One can place multiple buttons throughout the post. Easy Tweet Embed also helps your visitors tweet your content by embedding tweet buttons in the post. You can link different parts of a post and get them tweeted separately, thereby reaching a greater audience.

Show social proof with Flare/Digg Digg/"Sumome Share app:"

https://wordpress.org/plugins/flare/
https://wordpress.org/plugins/digg-digg/
http://sumome.com/app/share

Imagine that at the top of the page on your blog post, the number of shares it has already achieved on various social media platforms is clearly mentioned. It will give social proof to every user who visits it as to how popular the particular post is. Wouldn't a great number up there be a great boost for new users to share it too? Tools like Flare, Digg Digg or Sumome are meant for this purpose. While Flare keeps a record of total number of shares along with platform-wise shares (or Flares), Digg Digg only gives the platform-wise details and not the summed up proof figure. Personally I love using 'SumoMe'. These simple one-time installation tools can give you tremendous results in terms of generating web traffic.

Engage with Pay with a Tweet (http://www.paywithatweet.com/):

This is a simple tool that can help you garner an enormous number of tweets and retweets for your blog. By installing the "Pay with a Tweet" feature on your blog, you can ask your users to pay you by way of tweeting your content in exchange for viewing/downloading your content or other free stuff. I know for sure this one works because most of my Twitter community is addicted to retweeting some of the blogs so they can download the free ebooks or music they offer every now and then.

There's another plugin that I prefer using over "Pay with a Tweet." It's called "Social Locker" https://wordpress.org/plugins/social-locker/ .

So, employing these useful tips, along with the meticulous application of these Twitter tools, can enhance your blog's Twitter reach by leaps and bounds. Going viral via retweets has never been so simple!

If you have any specific query related to using Twitter for your business, please send me your queries via Twitter. Use @jr_sci to mention me and #ask as a hashtag.

Chapter 11

GOOGLE+

Google+ has just stepped into its third year and has already managed to draw some valuable attention towards itself. As of now, there are millions of people who have registered here and the family keeps expanding. Ever since it was launched, there has been some interesting news focusing around this social media website. Here are some fun facts about Google +, which I found out, well, in Google itself:

Google plus is a nerd's social gathering
About 60% of the people on Google plus claim to be "software developers" or "webmasters" or "software engineers." We can safely say that this is a nerd's paradise.

Relationship status is kept under wraps here
A report submitted by a third party website suggested that as many as 12,000 people on Google plus are "in a relationship," while 25,000 are "married" and only 19,000 people are "single." The majority of people on this social

media website have clearly dodged the mention of their relationship status.

It is unique in providing gender options
Unlike most other social media websites, Google plus provides more than two options in the "gender" section. You can choose either male, female or other.

Google plus is testosterone-charged
According to reports released by a third party website, Google plus has been highly dominated by the male population ever since it was launched. Unlike Facebook and Pinterest, which has an equal gathering of the ladies, Google plus is attended mostly by men. Reports claim that about 70% of the population here is masculine.

Believed to be a threat by China
Just after Google plus was launched, China was seemingly threatened by its potential, so they decided to block this platform for security and other reasons. They used the firewall system to block out Google+ in their country.

Google plus consists of a youthful population
Statistics have shown that most of the people on Google plus are about 25 to 34 years old. In fact, most of the people who log in every day are within that age range.

Chatting is fun in Google plus
Hangout is the name given to the chat feature on Google plus. It provides a video chatting facility, in which you can share videos and chat at the same time. It allows video conferencing with several people at once. Not only that, you can add a hat or a moustache to yourself digitally to make it even funnier. You really don't want to miss out on this one.

Men here are looking for love
Another interesting thing to learn here is that, out of all the people on Google plus, about 95% of those who claim to be "looking for love" are men. Source: minyanville.com

Google plus believes the more the merrier
You can add up to 5000 friends to your friend list on Google plus.

It loads faster
Google plus does not display any ads, and thus it loads faster, unlike Facebook and other social media platforms.

Google plus is like any other social media platform, yet it manages to be different from the rest. It is the only place where you can create your own circles and add your Google contacts smoothly.

Google plus has been one of the most talked about applications in recent times. It was believed to have taken over the fan following of Facebook, but that didn't happen initially. However, its simplicity and extensive features continues to draw in more and more people every day.

Chapter 12

Essential Tips To Use Google+ Effectively

Because of the complicated intricacies of Google Plus, many amateurs and professionals have tried to solve its various puzzles. Some just stumbled upon a cool way to work with Google Plus and others derived results after painful, consistent observation. Nevertheless, we all can benefit from these wonderful tips that I have summarized below.

Deactivate Auto-Upload Feature: Google+ automatically uploads photos or videos taken by some Android phones directly to Google+. Although it doesn't share them with any of your circles till you specify, still it congests a lot of your space, so it's advisable to turn the auto-upload feature off!

Add other profiles to Google+: This is an important tip as far as building online trust is concerned. Anyone trying to connect with you over the net wants to know you better, and what better way is there than connecting your Facebook, LinkedIn and Quora profiles right from your Google+ profile?

If clients know you on other social media platforms, such as Facebook, you can link your Google+ to your Facebook (or other sites) posts and that will help them trace you to Google+. It will also make it easier for them to share your Google+ posts. It enables you to engage through a wider network. Also, link your posts to other relevant older posts for reference.

Publish Sync: This is cool extension in Chrome. It can be installed to simply publish all your posts on Google+ to your other social profiles, such as Facebook, Twitter, LinkedIn, etc. You do not need to use a separate tool.

Format your content: Those **BOLD**, *italics* texts and bullet points might sound naive, but the truth is that the content you post on Google+ (or anywhere online, for that matter) is ranked by search engines on the basis of the number of links, mentions and interactions you get, and it is obvious that visually attractive posts will get more links, mentions and interactions.

Popular Google+ Formatting:

- *Word* = **Word**

- _Word_ = *Word*
- Tag People using @Name or +name
- Add videos, photos and links by dragging the links directly to the share box

Facebook Nostalgia: So you haven't gotten over your love for Facebook yet? Is it difficult to move on to Google+? *Picknzip.com* will export all your Facebook activity to Google+ in a flash so you don't feel like a newbie. Also, *Google+: Facebook Stylish* extension will give your Google+ profile a look very similar to the blue Facebook.

Google+ Black App: This is a genius app, a must have for Android; this is simply your very own Google+ but in black instead of white. Evidently, it also consumes less battery.

Native Gmail: This is another great extension in Chrome. It provides a new notification tab on your Google+ page for your Gmail updates, in addition to the regular one for the Google+ updates. Pretty cool, right?

Upload images instead of sharing: This gem of a tip tells you to simply download and then upload an image you find interesting, instead of simply sharing it. This ensures that the image is displayed in a larger format and is sure to grab more eyeballs. You can add your own comments or copy the ones in the previous post itself. Just don't forget to tag the person who posted it initially.

It is your own blog: No other social networking platform gives you the freedom to post long texts (really long indeed), images and videos as does Google+. So go ahead and make a blog out of your Google+ profile. You can share as much content as you want and in any form. You can even include links to your new posts, exactly like you would be able to do on a real blog, in order to become more visible.

Build email campaigns around your posts: This is a sure-shot way to reach audiences beyond the people in your circle. For this, all you need to do is create email campaigns about your posts on Google+. You can ask your subscribers to check out your latest post on Google+ like you do for your blog. If a couple of them share your post with their Google+ circle, it will reach an even wider audience.

Blocked Circle: Who doesn't need to block some nasty unwanted souls every once in a while? You will get this circle in red instead of the usual blue, so you can choose not to share any stuff with the folks you wish to avoid.

Use #hashtags and keywords you want to be associated with: Your Google+ profile is the one source of information about you that

Google will never go wrong about. So use the keywords and hashtags that you want to be associated with, not just in your posts but also in your profile entries and descriptions. Ever heard of an easier way of self-branding, eh?

Understand the concept of Communities: Communities on Google+ are self- motivated and active interest groups, unlike the groups and pages on Facebook that are largely governed by their admins. The best way to gain is by contributing, interacting and engaging. In simple words, "be active." You can even start your own community with a unique interest.

Find your way to Hangout: This unique feature of Google+ not only lets you interact with your friends in real time, but it also allows you to host live events or webinars. You can hold meetings, blog sessions, book clubs, Q & A sessions or even lectures. Find out how you can make it work for you.

Let's Talk About Increasing Google+ Engagement

Here are a few ways to increase engagement and help you get to the top of the charts:

Share and plus one

A great way of engaging is by making the effort to establish communication. Read other's blogs and post and plus one and share them. This will ensure that they read your posts and share them. Remember the reciprocation rule?

Follow
Follow relevant people and businesses. They will get a notification of the same and if they are interested in your business, they will begin to follow you.

Be visual
Post photos, videos and other visual data relevant to your business. This helps explain things better and attracts people who could be interested in you. Even make your cover picture relevant - a picture of the office or of the employees.

Use tags
Tag people, clients, businesses, etc. to connect better. They will plus one your post, share it and might even tag you in their posts. I have already showed you how to tag. Use +Name or @Name.

With these irresistible tips, you can engage with your audience better, create a great branding for yourself online, be an expert in media and Google+, and ultimately find your own different ways to work with this already enormous and yet growing space of Google+.

Whether you are a beginner, a social media enthusiast, a businessperson or anyone who wants to explore this realm, these tips will give you a head-start and a phenomenal insight into how to make the circles and +1s work for you!

Take my advice here. You cannot understand all of the entities and possibilities of a social network by only reading books. You need to get out there and try out every element by yourself. Take a note of your doubts and consult your friends who might be able to solve your problems.

Chapter 13

Google+ Tools to Improve Your Marketing

Read on to discover an assortment of tools (some are built-in, yet unknown) to be used with your Google+ profile or page to give your marketing strategy the boost it needs.

Auto Awesome Movie: This one's a rage for visual content marketing. This tool by Google+ creates movies using your photos and videos. It is really useful for startups and small businesses who can't invest in high-end video software and/or experts. It not only edits and filters content, but also adds music. You can also customize it by adding or deleting specific content. The movie you create might just make you the next sensation in the market.

Friend+Me (https://friendsplus.me/): This amazing tool can reduce your working time drastically as an online marketer. All you have to do is install this tool on your Google profile or page and associate it with your profiles on other social media platforms like Facebook, Twitter, LinkedIn, etc. It is a little pain to apply all of the settings for all of the different sites initially, but it is surely worth it. Now, every time you post content on Google+, it will automatically get posted across all associated platforms. Now that's what I call a smart move!

AllMyPlus (http://www.allmyplus.com/): This is a free website offering analysis services to one and all. It works especially for Google+ and records all the statistics associated with your profile or page. It is a great tool when you want to consider all your posts, shares, comments, +1s, etc. from a long time ago, and analyze them to understand the evolution of your profile or page. This site does just that and displays the results in the form of graphical and interactive media - right down to your most or least popular hours.

CircleCount (http://www.circlecount.com/): This is a website that lets you see the record of the most happening pages and profiles on Google+. It studies the journey of the pages right from inception up to today's date. Businesses can use these to keep track of a competitors' popularity and gain useful insight into the kind of followers they have, such as like nation-wise, gender-wise, occupation-wise, etc.

Chrome Do Share plugin: This one by Google is extremely handy for those who can't spent all of their time online. Just install this plug-in on your Chrome browser and you can schedule your Google+ posts to be posted whenever you want them to be posted, from your personal or brand profile. You can even schedule posts of content you find interesting while browsing. The only thing that you need to take care of is to ensure that Chrome browser is running at the scheduled time on your computer.

+Post Ads (http://www.google.com/+/brands/ads.html): Ads are the most popular form of marketing and are known to provide maximum converts, and this hell of a tool by Google+ creates advertisements out of your content and posts these ads across Google's various platforms. This is a great way to be visible way beyond one's circle in Google+. These ads are designed so that people can +1, comment, join a hangout while, let's say, simply googling.

Google Plus Brand Page Audit Tool
http://www.steadydemand.com/Google-Plus-Brand-Audit-Tool.php
This tool is by the analytics company Steady Demand. It is specifically made to study and analyze your brand page and check whether it is

complete in all respects and has all necessary extensions and plugins that might be useful based on your particular way of using your page.

NOD3x (http://nod3x.com/): This one is a Social Network Analysis (SNA) service. It is basically a semantic-based analytical tool and is particularly useful for Google+ and YouTube. It records and calculates the influence of a particular topic or keyword or hashtag in online media. It reports in the form of real-time graphs, based on information regarding gender, location, time, sentiment, etc.

Timing+ (http://timing.minimali.se/): As the name suggests, this tool will help you time your posts well. It analyzes the response to your last 100 posts and identifies suitable posting times for future posts. Just login and schedule your posts and you will reach a greater audience every time you post.

These simple, yet effective tools can walk the walk and talk the talk for you in your marketing agenda. The idea is to identify exactly what you need out from you're your tools to make your life and your business easier. Explore one or more of these, or all of them, according to what best suits you, and nothing will ever stand in the way of you and your marketing targets.

Chapter 14

FACEBOOK

Suppose you have a business or a creative page on Facebook and you want more engagement on that page to increase traffic and make your business or page more popular among people. What do you do? Simply buying Facebook ads or paid post boost is not your answer. You will need to work towards building an audience on Facebook organically. You will need to do some work and also will need a couple of strategies.

Your main idea is to get as many likes and comments as possible. The likes and comments of a person are visible to his friends. If one of his friends engages with your FB post, it will again reach the friends of his friend. That's how your post has the ability to go viral. Here are some sure-shot tips to increase Facebook engagement for your respective page.

Some Tips to Increase Facebook Engagement:

Include Videos

Make sure to make and format some informative videos which describe your Facebook page's purpose and what exactly you intend to do. This would be very helpful because today, in the age of YouTube and other visual media, it will surely keep people engaged.

You can also include some fun videos in your daily post content. People will react to and engage with your posts.

Hold Facebook Contests

This is one thing which will surely get people interested and engaged. Include weekly or daily contests on your page. People who have followed your page will come back to play those contests, which will keep them interested, and they will also check out the page's content.

Ask simple and interesting questions

Simply posting a link to an article won't do you any good. You need to act like a human being, even though you are posting as a company. Personalize each and every post. Include simple and engaging questions three to four times a day and let your fans answer them. There is another thing you can do - post some interesting sentences with blank spaces and let people fill in the blanks!

Sample posts by a soft drink company:

Do you like Coke with pizza, fried chicken or a burger?

I love to drink Coke with _____.

If the world gets rid of Coke, I will _____.

Coffee or Coke when you are stressed?

Share Funny photos

This is an awesome way to keep people engaged. Suppose you have shared a funny photo and you tell people to suggest a funny caption for that photo. People will have fun and it will be beneficial for you as well. Do this on a daily basis, which will ensure that people will come back to check for those funny photos daily! You should always ask your fans and followers to "like" or "share" it.

If you can't find any photos on your own, find some from other pages that have received a lot of post engagements. Use the same photo on your FB page. Find what's working if you don't have the time to test it yourself.

Promote on other Social Media

Social media such as Twitter and Quora have become very popular nowadays; you can provide links to your Twitter fan page or post questions on Quora. Quora also enables you to post on Facebook every time you answer a question. This will show your authority on a subject. Integrate them. Let your Facebook fans know that you are knowledgeable and an authority on that subject.

Include Quotes

People immediately relate to quotes when it resembles their lives, so make sure that you share some quotes by famous personalities or even normal quotes with pictures. This will engage fans and people who have come to visit your page. Who doesn't like a bit of inspiration? Quotes are the secret weapon that I use across all my social media channels to get engagement.

Customize Content

Sometimes it's beneficial to ask fans or people who have followed your page for relevant content. This will make people more engaged and they will be more than happy to provide you with ideas for content. When you inject their ideas onto your page they will feel good and it will increase your traffic also!

Reply to Fans

Many times people will post on your page asking you for certain things or to include some content on your page. Make sure to reply to each one of them. This will make people happy and they will certainly check out your page quite a number of times. Whenever someone comments on a picture or a video, try to reply.

Notice other pages

There are millions of pages on Facebook. Look for similar and popular pages and study their way of increasing engagement and traffic. You will be able to learn a lot from the techniques they use in managing their page. Copy your competitors. I would recommend this over innovation. It's the shortcut to success (if there is a shortcut), but you get my point, right? You need to look around for opportunities, see what's working for others and then use the same for your business.

Content posting time

The times you post matters a lot. People usually access Facebook during their free time, which is usually at night, so try to post between 7 p.m. and 12 a.m. Maximum numbers of people stay online during this time period and are most likely to notice the posts. You can also schedule your posts early in the morning when people check their mobile after waking up.

Promote your page

There is a new addition to Facebook known as "sponsored post," in which you can promote your page on Facebook by paying a nominal fee. This is not a very unique way for increasing engagement; nevertheless, you can try it. There's one important strategy you need to remember. Boost posts that have already received tons of engagement. Don't spend your money on posts that doesn't receive organic engagement. You will lose a lot of money that way. Again, see what's working organically and then boost your post to reach even a wider audience.

Post Giveaways

People love freebies. So if you can include free giveaways for people, they will be over the moon. You can ask them to share and like the offer posted and thus participate in the giveaway. This will not only lead to people who have followed your page liking and posting it, but the friends of fans who have not yet visited your page before will also start coming in.

If you don't have products to give away, collaborate with some other companies who are willing to offer a giveaway to your fans. You will find a lot of companies who are looking for promotion. It's a win-win for both parties.

Post Frequently

Your Facebook page's engagement also depends on the frequency of your posts. It has been noticed that pages with more frequent posts get more visitors than pages with a smaller number of posts, so be regular in your post timings, which will keep visitors interested.

Get a professional LOGO + Facebook Cover banner

Invest a little money on a good logo and a Facebook cover banner. It will make your business look more professional and authentic. You can find a designer on Fiverr.com for as little as $5. If you want to make your own banner, I recommend http://www.bannersnack.com/.

Follow new trends

The latest craze on Facebook right now is "hashtag marketing." Twitter is the king in "hashtag marketing," but Facebook is not far behind. Facebook has introduced hashtags like Twitter and Instagram. It helps your posts get discovered more easily. It defines the purpose of your posts at the same time.

One of the most effective techniques is, however, to ask people. It sounds like a simple thing to do, and yet many people tend to ignore it. You might think you will sound needy, but this is not the case. If you don't ask people to share, like or comment, they won't. It's just like shaking hands. If you move your hand forward, they will shake hands. If you don't, they won't.

These tips are not too exhaustive, but they will help you to a great extent in managing your page and increasing engagement on Facebook.

Chapter 15

Market Your Brand on Facebook

Networking is the premise for the inception of social media sites like Facebook. However, these past few years, Facebook has been more than just about reconnecting with old pals.

It's risen as a powerful marketing tool, for home-bakers and blue-chip companies alike. Every business strives to get more page likes, referrals and customers, but what are the ways in which you can promote and garner support for your business in a fool-proof way?

Read on to find out.

1. On a run to follow:

As Facebook introduced the "follow" system, traditional Facebook advertising continues its reign at the top of social media advertising. As with any social media website, your page might have a thousand likes; however, people might rule you out because of inaccessibility. A business has to circumnavigate. Before globalization, it was a matter of territory, and now it's across the web.

The new "follow" system of Facebook allows the people who "like" your page to regularly stay updated and follow the activity of your business. This might seem extremely fundamental and rudimentary, but one of the major attributes that buyers look for when looking up businesses online is reliability and accessibility.

The new "follow" button allows just that.

Once a user likes your page, they become followers of your business page, and your posts will appear on their Facebook news feed. What this leads to is more interaction with the brand and you, and a sustainable business is all about long-lasting relationships that blossom into brand-loyalty and referrals.

Bottomline:

1. Treat your fans and followers with respect. Do not spam them. Your primary aim should be to increase your brand awareness, not simply to get sales.
2. You need to get some followers before people start following you. **In other words, you need social proof**. In the beginning, you

might have to run a campaign using paid ads, giveaways, etc., to earn a few followers.

2. Facebook Open Graph:

Following, liking and posting statuses are just the beginning of the game. What makes a business truly successful is when entrepreneurs stay up to date with the interactions of their customers.

In 2010, Facebook launched its "Open Graph" API.

What the platform basically does is allow the business owner to monitor and collect information by connecting your website to Facebook. One week after its release, the new Open Graph plug-ins were already found on 50,000 websites.

Deciphering the working of the Open Graph is pretty simple. You can add buttons to your website, be it Live Stream, Like Box, or activity feed. What you essentially do by adding these buttons is an integration of your website to Facebook, and in simple words that means that your domain is an extension of a Facebook page, with all its personal touches, so you can keep your clients updated and satisfied.

Hire a developer to integrate Facebook Open graph if you are not tech savvy.

3. The spirit of competition goes a long way

Hosting a Facebook contest isn't just easy and fun, it shows the customer that you care and can loosen up. After all, who doesn't like sweepstakes and healthy competition?

One of the most successful contests hosted by a start-up company was held by Qwertee, a t-shirt designing company. The contest required people to like their page and send in an e-mail, and the lucky winners got limited edition t-shirts. Through this contest, Qwertee aimed to improve their fan base and reach 100,000 likes.

After running the contest for a couple of weeks, their page had more than a 110,000 likes, and the company is currently known for their exclusive, yet cheap t-shirts, but most importantly, their "win-win sweepstakes" contests.

The Breakdown: Although these contests cannot be hosted through Facebook itself, there are many useful third party apps that can be used to host the contest and the fans will be directed from the Facebook page to the application page.

Some of the most widely used ones are Pagemodo, Wishpond and Shortstack; however, wider options and templates for running a contest do come with a price. Search for "Giveaway app" on Facebook search bar. You will find a few free apps as well.

4. The old-school way:

You can never go wrong with advertisements. They are straight-forward, simple and attractive. We can thank Facebook for their classic sidebar advertising lined with the blue casing, which somehow pops up right when the user needs a cake or a custom gift bag.

These ads, also known as marketplaces, typically have a headline, an inline image, and a link following the click of the cursor. This click maybe to another domain or to a Facebook page itself.

Some of the positive things about Facebook Ads are that they are demographic-centric, and they show up right where and when the service or product might be needed. It allows for flexibility in your budget. If a smaller business needs an ad, Facebook has options to let you do that.

The real winners here are the split-ad testing and the built-in ad performance measurement tools. Ad testing involves multiple ad versions that can be run simultaneously to compare Ad designs.

Studies from Mashable.com show that the advertiser's total return on investment took in more than 131 billion dollars on the basis of impressions, and Facebook ads were clicked on 29% more often in 2013, and the ROI to investors was 58% higher than last year.

5. It pays to be sponsored

Sponsored stories are both simple and effective. While we're talking about sweet additives, it might seem more appealing to add that these are a more reliable way of advertising as well, and bingo.

Facebook Sponsored stories work in a simple manner, with the feeling being that when a friend likes a particular page for anything, it ends up as a story on your news feed.

However, the same concept extends to sponsored ones also, where the story will have an earlier date stamp with the word "sponsored" on it. Sponsored Stories can get preferred positioning and are capable of appearing in news feeds and on the right side bar, and the icing on the cake is that these are the only ad formats that are compatible on mobile devices.

Sponsored Ads can be created through the Promote Page option; however, a more powerful tool to create them is "Power Editor," where these stories can be attached to both your Facebook page and your domain.

Facebook claims that the "Click-Through Rate" for them is 46% higher and have more reliability. If a friend likes a page, chances are you will too, right?

With over tens of thousands of businesses promoting themselves on Facebook, these are just a few ways in which Facebook has grown and diversified to take into account the interests of small, medium and large businesses alike. With more innovative marketing techniques, Facebook seems to be in the spotlight thanks to connectivity, which is why tapping into this market is most lucrative.

In the next chapters, we will learn how Facebook has impacted everybody around us.

Chapter 16

Some Facebook Predictions for 2014

It's been ten years since Facebook was launched (on February 4, 2004). In these years, Facebook has gone from being just a random project to a multimillion dollar industry. It has over one hundred million users and is on the top of the social media chart. It is most likely that you too are part of this million dollar industry. Now, after a decade, what changes can Facebook users expect to see in the future? Let's find out!

1. Facebook grows - accepted in schools and offices
With the Facebook user-base ever-increasing, it will find its way onto the academic front. Teachers who currently use Google groups and emails to communicate with their students after school/college, will finally accept Facebook and share information there. While emails were considered more formal, Facebook is more advanced, user-friendly and makes sharing a lot

easier. For these reasons, it might even get acceptance in the workplace, such as possibly video conferencing on messenger replacing Google hangouts.

2. Facebook might buy other social networks/mobile apps

With Whatsapp and Snapchat already on the list of applications that Facebook wishes to buy, it seems like it will end up buying more apps to increase its user-base. We might just be headed to a future where Facebook will control most of our social networking apps and a Facebook account will be enough to access all of them, just like Google works now. It might purchase Vine, Pinterest, Instagram, etc. Who knows?

3. Facebook will replace search engines

With many people looking to Facebook for their daily dose of news because of its connection with news providers, it seems that Facebook will also become the platform for searching other information. If Facebook collaborates with information providers like Wikipedia or creates its own portal for discussing and sharing information, this will happen sooner than we'd expect.

4. Facebook marketing transforms
Facebook will have better ways to deal with ads and sponsored posts. Instead of sponsored posts spamming our news feed, we'll see a more content-based form of marketing. We'll see blogs, video ads and user-friendly information, instead of random "buy-our-product" type of ads. Facebook has already taken the first step with the 20% image/text rule. They are already going visual.

5. Transactions through Facebook
Facebook has a gifting feature which allows users to send and receive gifts through Facebook on occasions like birthdays. Commerce through Facebook will gain even more popularity with more similar features coming up.

6. Disappearing content
With internet content being ever-increasing and people getting hungry every day for even more information, this might give way to old content. This means Facebook content might start disappearing. Yup, you read that right! Facebook could start deleting old content on its own and probably even your old posts and shares will be deleted. Internet space will be used more judiciously. Well, it's just a prediction among

internet marketers for now, but let's see if it becomes a reality in the coming years.

Facebook is ever growing and recent predictions of it losing 80% of its users have been proven to be rubbish. Thus, it will soon cover an even larger space in the social media realm, without much competition. It might easily replace Google and every other search engine in the future.

Chapter 17

How Facebook Has Changed The World?

I have written this chapter not only to just to praise Facebook, but to show you the possibilities once can achieve with Facebook. After reading this chapter, I am sure you will come up with a lot of ideas on how you can use Facebook for your professional/personal use in your own unique way.

Gone are the days when social networking websites were used just for interacting, entertaining and rewinding. Today a social media website has the power to change the sociopolitical scenario of the world. People are using this platform to make their causes heard. According to a recent BBC documentary, Facebook has been the key factor in arranging protests in several parts of the world, including Arab, Egypt and Tunisia.

With more than 1.2 billion registered users worldwide, Facebook is currently the most crowded social network. Certainly it has the potential to cause a major stir in the face of world politics. From our daily life to our global alliances, Facebook has brought about some noteworthy changes in the past 10 years.

Donations for Tsunami and Earthquake in Japan: If it were not for Facebook, the word wouldn't have spread so far and wide. People were moved by the online campaigns, and the "donate via Facebook" option caused thousands of people to come out to help. Over $300,000 was raised via Facebook which made the Red Cross society reach the peak of their fund collection. You can raise money for any cause with Facebook. It's not rocket science. Many people have already done it as you can see.

Protests of the Middle East: The recent protests, famously called the "Arab Spring," received a viral outburst owing to the efforts of people gathering on Facebook to promote it. Without Facebook, rebel leaders would not have met like-minded people ready to be recruited. According to reports, Facebook has served a key role in overthrowing the dictatorial regimes of four nations, including Yemen, Libya, Tunisia and Egypt. It makes me wonder, how Facebook could be used as popular media to unite a group of individuals without holding any meetings and conferences.

Social isolation and narcissism are on the rise: According to a study conducted at Harvard University by Diana Tamir, the habit of self-disclosure on Facebook releases dopamine in the brain, which makes people addicted to its repeated usage. Furthermore, the study reveals that people who use Facebook more often are prone to self-isolation. Traits of narcissism have been observed in them as well.

Facebook created a new President: It is a well known fact that President Barack Obama used the internet to his advantage during his 2008 campaign. He made use of Facebook to draw attention to the youth. In recent days, more politicians from all over the world are making Facebook a tool for promoting their campaigns. It's like a drone in the hands of advertisers. They can promote any product to a laser-targeted audience.

Facebook provided a platform to entrepreneurs: Facebook advertiser Freddie Jansson said in an interview, *"A large part of companies' potential customers are there. Therefore, in my opinion, all companies should have a Facebook page (sic)."* Having an online platform to attract customers really helps, as is claimed by the owner of Beauty Planet - a Swedish cosmetic retailer. The company has received a significant increase in orders ever since they began marketing on Facebook. More and more entrepreneurs are using Facebook as a mode to find customers. It has never been so easy to build a business. Personally, I used Facebook to hire employees. I found thousands of prospects via Facebook. I can place an ad to find candidates based on which college they study, their work experience and so on.

It gave the world a reason to smile: According to a survey conducted in 2009 with 2600 college students at the University Of Texas, it was found that those who used Facebook regularly were generally happier with their lives. Recently, a similar survey was conducted at Cornwell University, which showed the same results. "Unlike a mirror, which reminds us who we really are and may have a negative effect on self-esteem if that image does match with our ideal, Facebook can show a positive version of ourselves," said the associate professor Jeffrey Hancock.

Dating made easier than ever before: According to a recent survey conducted by a dating website, as many as 48% of women do research before dating someone, while the percentage of men doing the same accounted for only 38%. Facebook profiles say a lot, don't they?

Facebook celebrated its tenth birthday on February 4, 2014. In these past ten years, it has created a legendary impact on our personal lives, as well as the world at large. We are sure more is yet to come as the years go by.

Chapter 18

Some Amazing Facebook Advertising Tips

Have you tried out Facebook advertising and haven't seen any good results? Or do you want to get started with advertising on Facebook but don't where to begin? Don't worry. You are not alone. We will be discussing a few tips that actually work. They are pretty short and simple, so you could start soon and see the results quickly!

I hope you are already aware of these basic principles:

- The more the CTR (click through rate) the less it will cost you per click (less CPC).
- Use different pictures. Pictures will impact the CTR.
- Use different headlines. Headlines will impact your CTR.
- Personalize each ad to a targeted audience.

- Your aim should be to increase the CTR.

If you are targeting lawyers in the US, create separate ads for each city. You can then personalize the headlines as:

- Lawyer in NY? Check XYZ
- Lawyer in LA? Check XYZ

One more important point to remember is to limit your daily budget while you are testing your ads. Keep it at $5.00 to $10.00. Once you find an ad that has a CTR of around 3% to 5%, increase your limit for that ad. You can then pause the rest of the ads.

1. **Call-to-action is your best friend**:
The title text that you provide for your Facebook ad plays the key role in bringing in an audience. The CTA is the blue text that is placed right at the top of your advertisement (HEADLINE). The more catchy and attractive your texts are the more people will click on it.

2. **Further segment your target audience**:
Having a target audience is the first step in marketing your product. Further segmentation of your target audience will make sure you receive more detailed and accurate information. This is true for niche products that require you to exclusively address a specific type of audience.

(See the example of the lawyers, which is listed above).

3. Use "Facebook Insights" feature to know your audience:

The Facebook Insights feature allows you to see which of your posts were the most liked by your audience and which ones were the least liked. This will help you to post similar stuff in that future which your target audience likes.

4. Make sure your campaigns are pre-scheduled:

Weekends are usually most recommended for campaigning. The hours and the time of the day will differ for different products. The best idea is to run your ads at different times during the day, so as to find out which time fetches you the maximum hits.

5. Use conversion tracking regularly:

Keep a record of the results generated by each and every advertisement. Facebook generally does not show which of your ads have generated what sort of result, but you can check the ROI often to see where the track record is headed.

6. Lead customers to your website:

You should make every area of your online presence known. Increasing traffic to your personal website will not only provide credibility, but will also create brand awareness.

It is absolutely necessary to give your fans other options apart from just your fan page.

7. The 20 percent rule:
Recently, Facebook has revised the guidelines for their ads that appear on the news feed. Any image based ad that goes out in the news feeds can have a text overlay, but the text should not take up more than 20% of the total image.

8. Lead your fans to multiple page-landing tabs:
A recently launched feature on Facebook allows you to direct your users to any part of your page, for example, wall, info, a particular image, etc. Use this feature to your advantage as you direct your fans to the exact place where you want them to be.

Tip: You can create custom HTML tabs using various apps on Facebook.

9. Use the data on Facebook for leverage:
The most interesting thing about marketing on Facebook is that you get an idea about the exact consumer base for your product, which you might not have known otherwise. Using the buyer's info you can get an idea about the kind of target audience you have for marketing in other variations.

10. Promote posts and grab more eyeballs:

Promoted posts will draw the attention of your target audience. It is the best way to start off your Facebook advertising campaign. However, make sure that you target your fans with your promoted posts so that their interactions prove more valuable to you. I have mentioned this earlier and I will state it here again. Promote posts that have performed well organically or else you will lose a lot of money.

11. Target desktop users to save money:

Unless you want to waste a lot of money, do not target mobile users. They do not convert as well as desktop users.

12. Newsfeed ads convert better than sidewide ads:

This is my personal opinion; however, I have talked to some people and all of them have found newsfeed ads to perform better than sidewide ads. Do test what works better for you.

13. Image borders:

Sometimes your ads will perform better when you have borders in your image. Work on your image and test 10-20 images for a single ad. I know people who will try 50-100 different images just to find that one image with maximum CTR. Then, they would pause the remaining ones and let the one with maximum CTR run.

I have a treat for my readers, a treat worth $96.00 per year. I am not sure if you are aware that I own a Facebook Retargeting Company. Here's the official website: http://munmi.org

Just email me (author@harsh.im) saying that you have brought my book and I will offer the Individual Package for FREE. It's value is $96.00 per year.

Here's how Facebook retargeting works:

Whenever someone clicks your ad and visits a landing page, they might not make the purchasing decision on their first visit. It takes time for a visitor to become a customer. With my service, you can re-target those who have previously clicked your ad again and again, until they make the decision to ultimately buy from you.

I am sure you have noticed EBay or Amazon ads on Facebook right after you have visited EBay or Amazon. They are using re-targeting to target anybody who has previously visited their website. You can have the same feature for your business with http://Munmi.org .

The best advice for marketing is that you keep

testing and tweaking all the options. You must solely discover what works best for you. Try out the above-mentioned pointers and you are sure to see a positive a positive ROI and growth.

CONCLUSION

A Note to My Readers

I have tried my best to make this book as informative as possible. I will improve this book in the next editions as I get more feedbacks and suggestions.

I love connecting with my readers on a personal level. You can always get in touch with me on social media or email me directly (author@harsh.im). I try my 100% to reply to each and everybody.

If you need to take away one advice from this book, then here it is:

If you do not interact and engage with other people they won't either. Hence, start interacting, engaging with others. Remember the law of reciprocation. It applies in every step of the way whether it's social media or personal relationships.

I always send my subscribers a FREE copy of my next book. Feel free to sign up to my list. Don't worry about spam. I hate spam as much as you do. This is your first step to connect with me.

Do sign up as a fan here: http://getaccess.me/no-seo-forever

Last but not the least, please REVIEW it on Amazon:

Nothing makes me happier than to see my reader's reviews. I go through every one of them. They motivate me every day to write better.

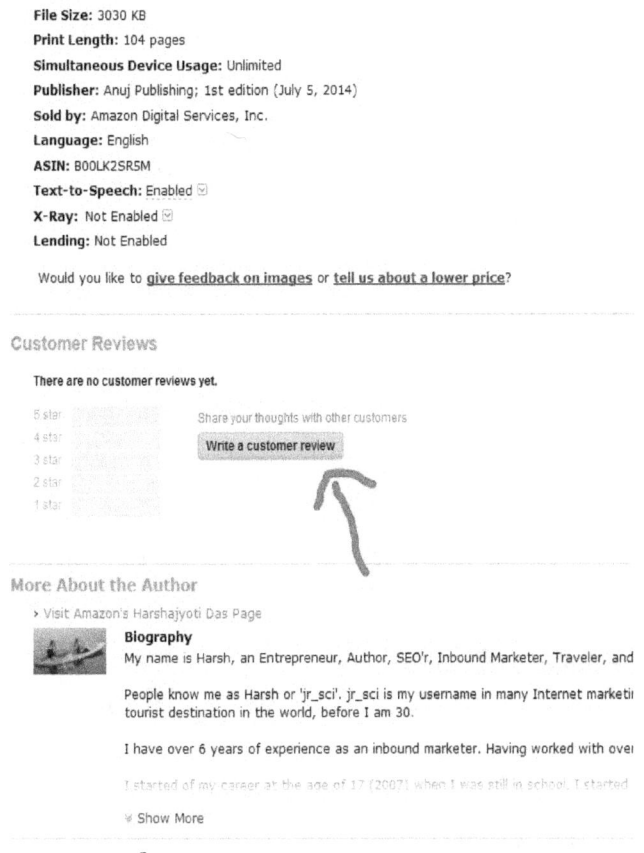

- Harsh

LET'S CONNECT!

Contact Info:

- **Fan Email:** author@harsh.im

- **Interview/guestposting/Press requests:** press@harsh.im

- **Amazon Author Profile:** http://www.amazon.com/author/harshajyotidas

- **Twitter:** http://twitter.com/jr_sci

- **Facebook:** https://www.facebook.com/harshajyotidas.author

- **LinkedIn:** http://in.linkedin.com/pub/harshajyoti-das/17/28b/52b

- **Google+:** https://plus.google.com/+HarshajyotiDas

Author Website: Harsh.Im

CEO at Munmi IT Solutions LLP:
Munmi.org

Founder of: FireYourMentor.com

ALSO BY THE AUTHOR

How To Write Content That Converts 600% More

http://amzn.to/1niszm5

ENGAGEMENT INTERACTION CONVERSION

http://amzn.to/1sWn9yB

ZERO ADVERTISING COST BLOG COMMENTING ROCKS

http://amzn.to/1rk4tej

THE ART OF BOOK MARKETING

http://amzn.to/1pcYOU5

BE THE GENIUS YOU WERE BORN TO BE

http://amzn.to/1onMX8C

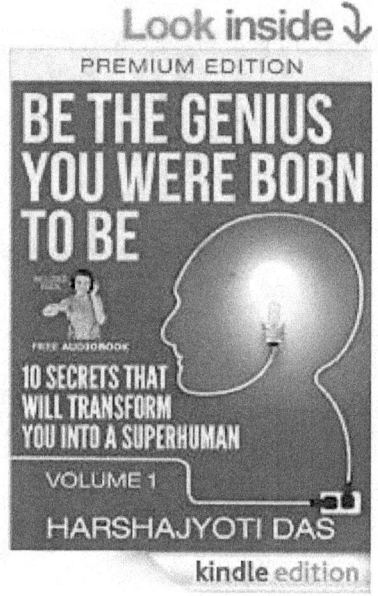

2014 by *Harshajyoti Das*

All rights reserved.

All Rights Reserved. No part of this publication may be reproduced in any form or by any means, including scanning, photocopying, or otherwise without prior written permission of the copyright holder.

Disclaimer and Terms of Use: The Author and Publisher has strived to be as accurate and complete as possible in the creation of this book, notwithstanding the fact that he does not warrant or represent at any time that the contents within are accurate due to the rapidly changing nature of the Internet. While all attempts have been made to verify information provided in this publication, the Author and Publisher assumes no responsibility for errors, omissions, or contrary interpretation of the subject matter herein. Any perceived slights of specific persons, peoples, or organizations are unintentional. In practical advice books, like anything else in life, there are no guarantees of results. Readers are cautioned to rely on their own judgment about their individual circumstances and act accordingly. This book is not intended for use as a source of legal, medical, business, accounting or financial advice. All readers are advised to seek services of competent professionals in the legal, medical, business, accounting, and finance fields.

First Published, 2014

www.ingramcontent.com/pod-product-compliance
Lightning Source LLC
Chambersburg PA
CBHW051712170526
45167CB00002B/633